Can I
Help You?

Can I Help You?

The Roadmap to Worldwide Peace
in the Twenty-First Century

FAROQUE QUAZI

iUniverse, Inc.
New York Lincoln Shanghai

Can I Help You?
The Roadmap to Worldwide Peace in the Twenty-First Century

iUniverse books may be ordered through booksellers or by contacting:

iUniverse
2021 Pine Lake Road, Suite 100
Lincoln, NE 68512
www.iuniverse.com
1-800-Authors (1-800-288-4677)

The views expressed in this work are solely those of the author and do not necessarily reflect the views of the publisher, and the publisher hereby disclaims any responsibility for them.
While every effort has been made to ensure the accuracy of the texts in this proposal, they cannot be taken as official legal documents.

ISBN-13: 978-0-595-42262-3 (pbk)
ISBN-13: 978-0-595-86598-7 (ebk)
ISBN-10: 0-595-42262-4 (pbk)
ISBN-10: 0-595-86598-4 (ebk)

Printed in the United States of America

How might we establish a Global Defense Department (GDD) at the United Nations? The answer lies within the proposal set forth in these pages.

I DEDICATE THIS BOOK to my dad and mom; they raised me to be a very strong, independent individual.

Contents

Acknowledgments

Thanks to my wife and our two children who gave me spare time to write this World Wide Peace proposal.

Special thanks to BBC *News World Editions*, *Voice of America*, and the Microsoft Corporation.

Introduction

LIKE MANY OF YOU, I am a simple, ordinary member of the working class who longs for world peace. Here in my book, you will learn of my ideas about how it can be achieved. Of course, these days, there are many books available on world peace, war, defense, and terrorism, but my book stands alone because its central idea is the establishment of the *GDD*, the *Global Defense Department.*

The GDD is a unique concept whose sole purpose is establishing peace between nations. To obtain a good understanding of this concept, I recommend that you read the entire book from start to finish. If you only scan the artwork, you might mistakenly think the subject matter is not intended for the adult reader. While it's true that most of the artwork is meant for a young readership, perhaps age twelve and up, the book is intended for an adult audience as well. You will notice also that the chapters are short; this feature, like the artwork, is because of my interest in reaching young readers.

When a country is in the middle of a war or suffers a sudden terrorists attack, working class individuals like you and I suffer more than others do. I speak from experience. When I was only seven years old, I lived in the midst of war, violence, and terrorist attacks.

Because of the horror of these experiences and my desire that other children not be forced to suffer as I did, I will donate one half of all the money I receive from the sales of this book to the GDD project. It's also my intent to print this book in all languages and distribute it worldwide. The other half of the proceeds will go to the WorldTEAM project—the Global Community Center (GCC)—which I am presently working on. Therefore, 100 % of the proceeds will be used for global peace. Please assist me in initiating the GDD and GCC projects by purchasing copies and giving them to your family and friends. You will not be making me rich; you will be spending your money for yourself, for global defense, for peace, and for future generations who will live peacefully on this earth.

Thank you!

The idea of a Global Defense Department (GDD) is mine only, and because America gives me freedom of speech, it is my duty to offer it to the world. God bless the United States of America and our World!

1

Who Should Read This Book?

THE WORLD

WE LEARN A LOT OF THINGS AT SCHOOLS, colleges, and universities. But no one teaches the reality or adventure of human life on earth. Many of us do not have any long, intermediate, or short-term goals. We all know how to dream, but we do not know how to make a road map to achieve our dreams. And we do not know how to do the hard work necessary. Success in life is difficult, but with the right preparation and persistence, we can all achieve more and have a better balance in the physical, work, family, financial, social, and spiritual areas of our lives.

We are citizens of our birthplaces on earth. Most of the time, our accomplishments in life depend on the environment in which we grew up. Consequently, it is very important for us to be in the right atmosphere. Any country can construct such an environment by setting up a good system and creating rules for its citizens, and when it does, most of the people of those nations will be more successful and produce better results for their country and for themselves.

My GDD proposal is aimed at establishing peace between countries by way of making new international rules and regulations at the United Nations. If all members of UN accept the proposal, then all world civilization will be affected for the good. Therefore, everyone on earth, from age twelve and up, should read this book.

2

The Problem Statement

ADAPTATION TO CHANGE is our key to improvement. If we do not adapt to the changes that are coming upon us, we will not be enriched by them. All-successful businesses accept change to improve their industries. The coming of the computer and the Internet changed our business model, and it is the voice of the citizenry through protest and voting that will make lawful changes in our culture.

We can destroy old weapons and technology with advanced weapons and new technology, but our new weapons cannot wipe out terrorism. Only by influencing the mind of the terrorist can we bring an end to this violence.

Let us imagine the entire world as one virtual country, and let us imagine that the name of that country is The United Nations. *In order to protect the citizens of this imaginary country, we have called the United Nations in the twenty-first century, our earth needs the GDD.*

Today's computer, satellite, communication, networking, and Internet technology make it possible for us to monitor the whole world from one location. No locations on earth are unknown to us anymore. The entire earth is already mapped, and all lands are owned by some country. Unclaimed lands do not exist anywhere in this world.

In order for us to survive well into the twenty-first century, all citizens on earth must respect each other's individuality. No two human fingerprints are the same. We all are different, and we all have different opinions because we have each been created with different versions of "software."

Countries go to war and use destructive weapons and terrorism because they have differing opinions on some crucial issue. Their leaders sometimes start war to demonstrate the power of their uniformed troops, and the power of their weapons. When a country does not have advanced weapons, it resorts to terrorism in order to destroy the superpowers.

We could transfer all of the troops and weapons belonging to the United Nations member countries to the GDD at the UN. With One World/One Nation, and with a global defense department in the United Nations, I believe that we can stop terrorism and war. The united obedience of all humans on earth to laws and regulations would guarantee a peaceful life for us and for future generations.

Today each country has its own department of defense that guards its territory and citizens. When a country can put together a stronger defense technology than any other country, that nation becomes the superpower on this earth.

It is human nature to want to be the best. One player confronts another in a game. One company competes with another company. One executive enters a contest with another, and so on. Similarly, every country tries to build the best defense system for its own interests and to protect its citizen and its region, and sometimes it becomes aggressive and goes after what does not belong to it.

Competition might be acceptable between two players or two companies, but in my opinion, when two countries enter the contest for superpower status, and build destructive, secret weapons, the result is terrifying. *We cannot stop this competitive behavior because it is one of the most powerful characteristics of human beings.*

The best player never wants another to take his position. Likewise, superpower countries by no means want other nations to take their places or become better than themselves by any means, and especially not by building destructive, mysterious weapons and technology. History has shown us that mutual fear is one of the principal motivations for war. In a battle, the citizens of all countries involved suffer in different ways. Both uniformed troops and innocent citizens die. Together, by putting the GDD at the United Nations we can end these crisis situations.

The GDD will also lead to a greater sense of brotherhood and sisterhood in the world community. A person, a company, or a country can improve by accepting or copying proven ideas from others. The GDD proposal is an innovative idea that will make it possible for all countries working together to establish worldwide peace in the twenty-first century.

So it is time to stop complaining and take action! As you can see, my vision is to launch GDD at the United Nations. *For worldwide peace, unity is not an option but an obligation.* Superpower countries have both the technology and the defense power to monitor and manage such a department. Every country in the world will have the opportunity to put its ideas on the table and become part of the GDD.

The biggest obstacles to our uniting in a common defense are:

- Nationalism,

- Racism,

- Religious animosity,

- Private and corporate self-interest,

- Fear.

People have loyalties to their groups over and above that which they have for world peace. If we can manage this problem, we will have gone a long way toward uniting world civilizations, avoiding war and violence, and stopping global terrorism.

The GDD layout at the UN will make us partners within the world community and enable us to support each other in curbing twenty-first century global war and terrorism crises.

A caveat: If any superpower nation individually initiates the GDD project on its own, within its own department of defense, the rest of the world will believe that that country is interested in other native soils and resources, and as a result, will not cooperate with the superpower's efforts. Because of this, the GDD initiative must be started as a joint effort in the United Nations.

The GDD is an enormous project. *We*—you and I—must work as one for its success in the twenty-first century. I propose that we join together and work as one with the entire world's civilizations.

"How do we safeguard our nation from war, violence, and terrorist attacks?"

To Find the Answer—Please read the entire proposal ...

3

The GDD is Unique

THE GDD CONCEPT does not exist anywhere in the United States or the world. It is not a request for the United Nations to play a more active role in day-to-day worldwide defense issues. Each nation will be able to make its own intellectual decisions, and will know what is best for its own country. But through the UN, each will establish a straightforward connection, networking with all UN member countries on the subject of global terrorisms and wars.

The Global Defense Department will guard world culture and every nation on earth. It is also a long-term, comprehensive global defense development strategy that will remove barriers to growth throughout the world. The United States government has an interest in or relations with almost every nation on earth. It is *the* best-known country for helping all over the world when help is needed.

Adaptation: The GDD will assist the world's future generations in learning and working with all United Nations member countries, cultures, and peoples. It will promote innovation aimed at preparing our world for growth and success in a global economy. The GDD will assist in coordinating and monitoring the defense of all nations from one central location. In this way we can protect the culture, traditions, and territory of every country on earth.

4

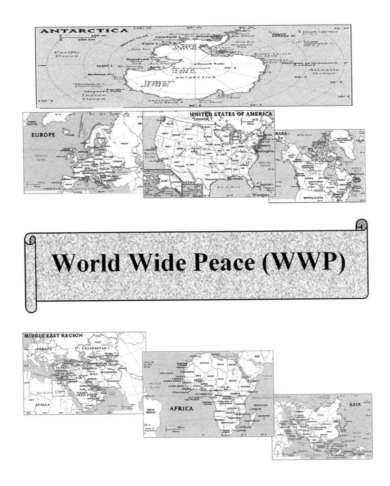

World Wide Peace (WWP)

I ALWAYS WANTED TO DO SOMETHING for the innocent civilians who die in sudden terrorist attacks and in the global war against terrorism. A very small percentage of these people are part of a terrorist group or are promoting war. Instead, *they are victims.* To join with me to help those who may yet suffer from terrorism and war, please read this proposal. It may prove to benefit you in some personal way.

The GDD is one of the best ways to protect every culture and people of our earth. It will command universal respect that cuts across ethnic, religious and cultural divisions and carry a message that we can all relate to. It will inspire unity and spread the simple message of understanding and respect for diverse opinions.

The GDD will develop a world culture of human unity and increase everyone's knowledge and wisdom. Remember, knowledge is power. *What you learn in this book will help you engage with the world community in sharing opinions and adopting good ideas.*

This proposal is written for the benefit of all cultures and humans on earth. As an element of earth, every nation has the right to freedom, and each nation must take responsibility and be accountable for its own actions, even as all GDD leaders must act according to international law.

5

GDD Capability

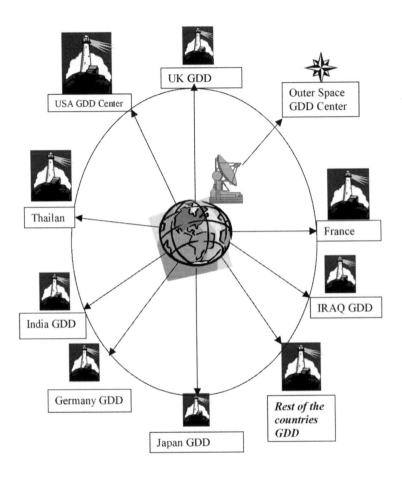

Worldwide GDD Center

GLOBAL DEFENSE DEPARTMENT MONITORING CENTERS will be set up all around the world and in outer space. Every nation on earth will network through these centers. No new resources will be needed because the GDD will use presently existing Internet and satellite technology to "wire" the world.

"How can we work with the leaders of the superpower countries at the United Nations to avoid conflicts?"

To find the answer, please read the entire proposal …

6

GDD Partners

THE INITIAL PARTNERS IN THE GDD will be the members of the United Nations Security Council. The GDD will initiate unity among governments and place international troops around the globe.

In the twenty-first century, our knowledge, habitual culture, and weapons of defense are rapidly changing. The changes are occurring so quickly that we are unable to protect our nations in the traditional ways from terrorist attacks and war. The GDD will create an atmosphere to work as a TEAM, not only in the United States of America but also with all countries in the world's defense department.

7

GDD Goals

THESE ARE THE GOALS that the GDD will enable us to achieve:

1. The elevation of each nation's department of defense.

2.   The strengthening and betterment of relationships between all United Nations member countries.

3.   The Power of Unity. Together we can make the world a better place to live, a better place to do business, and we can make a better future for our selves and the following generations.

Accomplishing these goals, the United Nations GDD will be one of the world's most highly honored means in the twenty-first century for achieving worldwide defense and peace.

Comparing the power of America to the rest of the world—I believe that *only* United States of America has the strength to initiate a project like the GDD, and through it achieve worldwide peace, avoid war and violence, and stop global terrorism.

8

The GDD Vision

The GDD scales of justice

THE GDD PROPOSAL WILL ESTABLISH peace by extending an invitation to all world civilizations without discrimination as to race, religion, creed, or color. It will break barriers between countries and cultures. Also, it will stop the blaming and finger pointing between nations and their leaders.

We teach our kids at school not to start fights or use weapons, and we educate them to use their words and knowledge to resolve all disagreements with others. However, when adults come to a disagreement about peace on earth, we do not abide by our own words. Consequently, we must make ourselves as accountable for behaving in a civilized manner as we make our children.

All uniformed troops from every country in the world will work for the GDD, united to establish peace without wars, to stop terrorism, armed conflicts, fuel crises, and nuclear power struggles. No war and no terrorism should exist on earth. *Superpower countries and Western society have successfully marketed the computer and Internet in the last quarter of the twentieth century, and now the challenge is to introduce this GDD concept in twenty-first century to the entire world.*

GDD will establish the principle of human rights, the rule of international law, freedom of movement, assembly, and association, freedom of religion and international peace and harmony. *To insure that these rules and regulations are formulated evenhandedly, they will be set up by selected officials from every country in the world.*

This GDD concept will move each country's defense power to the United Nations. *No single country will be responsible to protect its regions or citizens from international conflict. Only the GDD at the United Nation will take the responsibility for world defense.*

Once the GDD proposal is accepted by the U.S. State Department and the United Nations Security Council members, world leaders will set up the GDD's mission. *Since the president of United States of America has the ability to initiate war against terrorism and violence, it is my assumption that our president also has the power to launch the GDD process at the UN in behalf of worldwide peace.* I am sure our president and U.S. Department of States will give attention to the GDD project if we the people all lift our voices in its favor.

It is our duty to act in a caring manner for all of earth's creation. We pray for the defeat of extremism and terrorism. We pray for the safety and security of all inhabitants of our planet. We pray that inter-faith harmony and cooperation will finally prevail both in the United States and all around the globe.

What we are facing is a multi-national crisis that can be addressed only by multi-national solutions such as the GDD will be able to provide. Only in this way can we prevent terrorism, violence, and war.

"What is the relation between war and terrorism?"

To Find the Answer, please read this entire proposal …

9

The GDD Concept

Global Defense Department (GDD)

THE IDEA IS ONE WORLD, ONE NATION, and one Global Defense Department (GDD) at the national level. *In order to stop terrorist activity, violence and war in our world, we need an excellent plan, not excellent weapons.* We should have only one army, air force, and navy on earth to protect all countries. The name of the department overseeing these forces would be the Global Defense Department, a division of World Wide Peace at the United Nations. *The GDD's primary responsibility will be to protect each nation's region, people, identity, and interests from the depredations of other nations.*

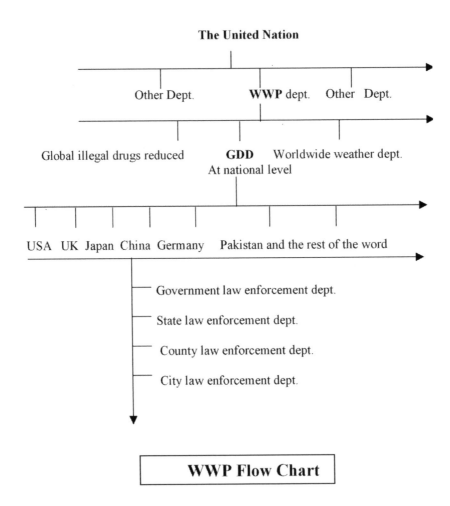

The United Nation

Other Dept.   **WWP** dept.   Other Dept.

Global illegal drugs reduced   **GDD**   Worldwide weather dept.
At national level

USA UK Japan China Germany   Pakistan and the rest of the word

Government law enforcement dept.

State law enforcement dept.

County law enforcement dept.

City law enforcement dept.

WWP Flow Chart

Each nation's leader now works hard to improve its own defense powers and technology. But in fact, some leaders don't care about other countries and their peoples, cultures, traditions, and values. The Creator of our universe will not come to earth to take care of world leaders, because he or she did not divide our earth into different nations. It was human leaders who divided our earth into countries. That is the reason that humans need to establish the GDD to protect our earth. Without the GDD, there is a vacuum in defense power all the way to the top.

But in reality, from antiquity, the nations have been constantly vying to fill that vacuum. It has always been filled by some nation, and though the United States of America fills it now, every country's leader wants to hold the superpower defense title. And as always, the method lies in the power of new advanced weaponry and technology.

Some of the wars on earth have started because of weapons competition; a nation so fears the increasing power of another that it strikes out. Some Western countries spend one third of their national budget on defense systems. In fact, these nations' weapons of mass destruction have been created for the very purpose of stopping terrorism and violence. When other nations try to follow the Western countries' footsteps by creating their own weapons of mass destruction, it starts war, violence, and terrorism. Together we can fix this crisis at the GDD.

10

Will the GDD Concept Work? How Can We be Sure?

The Global Defense Department (GDD) proposal

THINK OF THIS. Superpower countries have citizens that come from different parts of the world and live mutually in big cities. Each of these large cities has only one police department, not separate police departments for each of its ethnic populations. All citizens pay taxes that support only one police department. When a citizen needs help, he calls the *city* police department, not the Hispanic Police Department or the Italian Police Department.

This concept has been functioning in large cities for more than a hundred years, so we can see that it is a proven model that is already established. Superpower countries have already proven that they can manage diverse ethnic populations under one police department and one set of rules and laws.

Following this model, I believe the GDD would be able to manage all countries' defenses using advanced weapons and technology for worldwide peace.

11

How Can We Bring the GDD into Being?

Teamwork and Partnership with Other Nations

WE ARE LIVING IN A GLOBAL WORLD ECONOMY. We need universal teamwork and partnership with other nations to stop war and global terrorism. *The GDD project must be initiated as teamwork at the United Nations, not anywhere else in the world.*

Task 1. The United State's State Department needs to approve the GDD project.

Task 2. Each country's Security Council Members need to get together at the United Nations and open two new departments called WWP and GDD.

Task 3. All Security Council member nations must transfer their defense department to the GDD. In other words, every defense department must merge with every other country's defense department at the UN.

Each country's defense department workers now become employees of the GDD. Each country transfers its national defense budget to the GDD. The GDD takes an inventory of all employees and all weapons. Then it becomes the GDD's job to manage all employees, international troops, and advanced weaponry.

By creating the WWP & GDD, superpower countries will remain independent in their respective fields of advanced science, technology, value of currency, government management style and power, and in their educated and intelligent citizenry, etc.

Superpower citizens do not feel comfortable fighting alone or in declaring war with other countries to resolve other nations' local government or weapon problems. Currently, superpower citizens award these headaches to their president, leader, or king alone. I assume our superpower countries' leaders spend the greater part of their time every day on war, weapons of mass destruction, and terrorism, not to mention lots of sleepless night. *That is one of the reasons that superpower countries will be eager to combine defense departments in the GDD; these world issues can then be handled by an international team.*

When above tasks are completed, we will have accomplished the following:

a. Each superpower country's defense system (weapons and international troops) is now bigger and stronger because they are working as a united force.

b. Western countries now do not need to originate advanced weaponry alone.

c. Each nation as part of every other nation joined as one will be unable to declare war on the others.

If we can accomplish tasks 1 to 3, then we have a huge chance of success in the GDD concept. *Truly, only present superpower countries on earth can compose the GDD proposal successfully via exceptional planning, advanced weaponry, and advanced technology.* I do not believe any other countries in the world can or should take the first step toward the GDD.

Task 4. The GDD will advertise their accomplishment through every TV, radio, and newspaper system on earth for one year, and all humans on earth will be continually kept apprised of the GDD's existence and progress at the UN.

Task 5. The GDD will mail letters to all United Nation member or non-member countries' presidents, kings, queens, and leaders advising them regarding the procedures for merging their defense departments with the GDD. Each country's defense department will become a member. Its own people will work for its merged defense department, but they will be employees of the GDD. Each nation will transfer its national defense budget to the GDD for advanced protection, and as a result, each country's defense department will be more robust than it was when it stood alone.

I think most of the countries in our world will join quietly with the GDD, because all superpower countries have already become a part of the larger United Nations. Once the GDD gets support from a majority of nations, it will be easy to bring in those who were at first reluctant to join.

Are You Hunting for Worldwide Peace?

You will find it by reading the rest of this proposal.

12

Why the Citizens of the Superpower Countries Will Support the GDD, and What Benefits They Will Receive ...

Expanding Horizons

THE GREAT INCREASE IN TRAVEL AND COMMUNICATIONS has greatly expanded our cultural horizons, but it has shrunk our security. Once two great oceans protected us here in the United States from terrorism and war. Though they still offer some protection, we are much more vulnerable than we once were. That means that for our own good, we must do something else to shield our citizens from danger. This century has gotten off to a bad start and our young men and women are dying overseas. And yet terrorism increases. So what can we do? This is where the GDD comes in. With the GDD in place:

1. There will be no war between superpowers and least developed countries. That means superpower countries' uniformed troops do not go to war to least developed countries as a first defense. So we can save our weapons and troops' (our children's) lives.

2. When a least developed country faces an internal political issue between their citizens, or an external conflict, the president or opposing party's leader will not call the superpower country's president asking for advanced weapons and troops. They will call the GDD for help, because such matters will be the GDD's responsibility.

3. Superpower countries' presidents and citizens will have more peace of mind at home and overseas. There will be no particular countries to blame for war, and it will stop terrorist attacks and violence.

4. There will be a greater chance for economic development among the nations and in the superpowers. Every company's success depends on its employees. Similarly, superpower countries need outstanding and intelligent people from all over the word. If a country can offer a better and more peaceful place to live, then intelligent people from everywhere will want to live in that country. These bright people flowing into a nation will automatically build the nation economically and culturally.

13

What Benefit Will Third World Countries Receive from the GDD?

Peace of mind

THE GDD WILL PROVIDE SUPERPOWER PROTECTION for all third world countries. There will be no more fear of Western society's advance in weapons, technology, and uniformed troops. All international troops from all over the word will work as a team at GDD to protect our one nation on earth. There will be no reason to hide advance weapons from each other.

This means that every nation will be able to provide greater opportunities for normal human activities, education, family life, and so on.

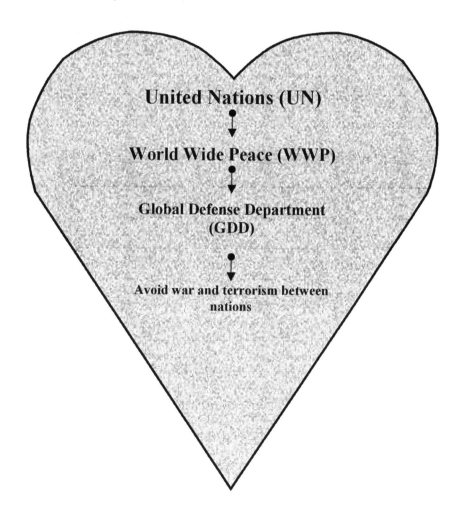

The most important thing in this life is to help others to win. Even if that means slowing down and changing our own pace.

14

Where Will the GDD Budget Come From?

The startup money will come from:

1. Defense grants from the superpower countries …

2. Each nation's department of defense budget …

3. Readers like you from all over the word …

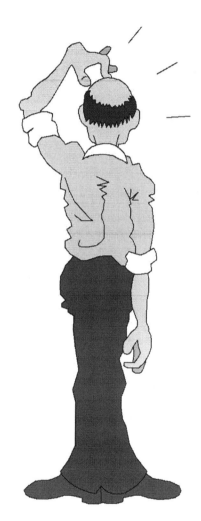

"I'm Confused! Why do terrorists come from the Middle East?"

To Find the Answer—Please read the entire proposal …

15

Searching History

FAR, FAR BACK IN TIME, humans constructed weapons to kill animals for food and to protect themselves from the violence of animals and other humans. Then came war. These weapons were limited by their technology and were less destructive than those we have today. They did fight over territory, and even in the earliest periods of recorded history, expensive real estate and logistical problems of transporting troops and weapons and food arose. Even in antiquity, they were confronted with the problems posed by terrorism.

When we analyze the more recent wars—the wars of the past two-centuries—we see that they were ferocious and took huge numbers of lives, wreaking havoc on land and property. Way back in those old days, a country's leader might declare war to increase his or her country's property and treasure, or to break away and become an independent nation. Sometimes it still happens that way. But now, many wars start for other reasons, and often, the reason is fear of another's nation's superior weapons and intentions.

There is a long history of nations ruling wide reaches of territory with new weapons and technology. First, wooden spears, then copper weapons, then bronze, and after that iron weapons gave nations advantages over other nations. In the last thousand years, the French, then the British, and after them the Germans, and then the Soviets dominated large areas with the power of sophisticated weaponry. Now they have lost the superpower titles to the United States, and in World War II, Germany, and during the Cold War, the Soviets have lost human support.

War produces a backlash. By nature, human beings are revolted at being placed under the rule of gunpoint. That means that through advanced weapon-power, a nation can get everything from another nation *except true support and respect!* When nations do not support and respect each other, good relations between them will not endure. *But good relationships could be achieved through care and support via the GDD.*

When a super-power country uses advanced weapons against another nation to achieve its interests, it might temporarily win, but in the process it will create a devoted group of terrorists from that defeated country. This, of course, has an effect on the entire world community. Many terrorists do not have to worry about property or life because in the preceding war, they have lost everything. Not only so, these terrorists can also find support from many activist groups in the world. *So, we can see that terrorism is the side effect of war.*

Who are the individuals in these terrorist groups? Identifying them is one of the most difficult jobs in the twenty-first century; they have normal lifestyles and do not stand out. If we cannot locate them, we cannot bring them to justice. And they are spread all over the world. Terrorists are normal, intelligent human beings who have no weapons to fight with, except that most advanced computer on earth—the human brain. In a superpower country, a human brain invents advanced weapons of war. Similarly, a non-superpower terrorist uses the brain in other ways to attack and destroy. So this becomes a game of human brainpower between nations and terrorists. And as we know, the human mind is very unpredictable and works mysteriously. Identifying terrorists has been an on-going, non-stop process, both in the past and now in the twenty-first century.

Normally, terrorists are not after uniformed troops or advanced weapons because they do not have the weapons or technology to compete with them. Without proper weapons or technology, it is not possible for them to get into the restricted areas. So the easy target is the every day person and place. As a result, they kill innocent people; they destroy real estate, transportation, communications, economy, businesses—things humans use everyday. Sometimes it takes years to recover from a terrorist attack and sometimes the loses are not recoverable at all.

A powerful nation may win in a conventional war, but because terrorism is often really a backlash, stopping it is very difficult and expensive.

Instead of just trying to find and monitor existing terrorists, we need to stop creating them. We need to have a process that will not create the backlash that puts terrorists in action 24/7, 365 days a year, all over the world.

Note: Please visit your local bookstore, library, or search Internet for information on specific precedents in war and terrorism.

Are you searching to find why terrorists attack superpower nations?

To Find the Answer—Please read the entire proposal ...

16

What War and Terrorism Does to Us

WAR AND TERRORISM INTERRUPTS the normal, peaceful life of the individual. It drives the public into previously unknown and uncomfortable life styles. It costs lives, ruins economy, damages real estate, and harms the environment of Mother Nature. As such, war and terrorism are not routes toward unity and establishing peace between nations.

Earth—this is where, by the grace of God, we all belong. There can never be any excuse for taking an innocent life via initiating war or acts of terrorism. What we need in our troubled world more than ever before is to stick to the middle road and balanced way of life. The GDD based in the United Nations will aid us in holding to the middle road.

The GDD proposal at the United Nations will begin an interfaith partnership with global culture. Members of GDD committee at UN will create the first written constitution for each nation's protection and safety. They will recommend to all nations and cultures that they bring every conflict to a conclusion and justice in a peaceful manner. GDD will use the full power of world media to broadcast their message worldwide.

17

The Threat from Weapons of Mass Destruction

WESTERN NATIONS ARE THE ONES who spend one third of their national budgets to create weapons of mass destruction in order to fight against global terrorism and other crises in the world. But perhaps we should ask: are the world's great superpowers initiating war in order to stop global terrorism, or are they doing it to keep the title, "superpower country"? This is a hard question to answer, but an important one to think about.

The American defense department is the best in the world. We Americans are the leaders of the world in advanced weaponry and technology in the twenty-first century. And other Western nations share in this sophisticated technology. It will take the less advanced nations at least another century to come to the place where American defense is now. Therefore, the countries of the globe are afraid of the more affluent Western countries. Some oil-rich Middle East countries are trying to advance their defense and become as strong as the Western nations. In the twenty-first century as in the past, this competition creates great conflict.
.

In today's global economy and culture, we desperately need a global solution like the GDD. Western countries' advanced defense departments could grow, learn, and better serve the worldwide communities. The WWP and GDD at the UN will establish unity of all American citizens with the global society in the twenty-first century.

18

Mother Nature

HUMANS HAVE BEEN SEARCHING FOR LIFE ON OTHER PLANETS for centuries, but without success. Earth-like environments may not exist anywhere in space. The formation of Mother Nature here on earth, the natural environment that we are enjoying every moment—all this began to develop six billion years ago. Whether we have faith in God or not, some superpower created all this that we now enjoy. All this—the sun, moon, earth, and wonderful Mother Nature are made just for us. We cannot survive outside of Mother Nature—not without artificial help.

How humanity originated here on earth or elsewhere in this universe is a very good question, and scientists should keep trying to find the answer. Humans are the most intelligent species on earth, and we at least should try. There are no animals that have the intelligence to protect or destroy Mother Nature—*except* humans. And now, with advanced weapons, *it takes only a few minutes to destroy a nice home that it has taken years to build.* Or the block on which the house sits, or the entire city. I have no doubt that Earth is one of the most amazing and beautiful things in this universe, and that it is our job to protect it and Mother Nature.

As far as we know, earth is the only place in the universe where we can live comfortably without any modification of the environment. And yet we destroy that environment. When someone forces destruction on a particular region, it not only destroys that region, but it also harms the environment globally. Using very advanced weapons, we are destroying Mother Nature. Every year, companies make new models of their products—advanced and better cars, airplanes, and appliances. Similarly, every year someone is developing new and advanced weapons. And those secret advanced weapons are now and will in the future be used to destroy some part of our earth and our beautiful Mother Nature. Unfortunate human beings, animals, and trees are dying and will die. We must do something about this. Together, let's save this wonderful environment that our Creator created for us six billion years ago.

Are You Searching the Internet for a Global Peace solution?

To find the answer, please read this entire proposal …

19

The Journey of a Lifetime

THE HUMAN JOURNEY THROUGH TIME has been a very long, hard one made up of thousands of generations.

Under the skin, we all are from one human origin or template. As a result, all humans on earth are actually one family. This means that we should be united and not divided. Rules and regulations setup by the GDD will help many to open their eyes and minds to this.

The only way we can achieve peace deep inside our hearts is to unite with each other. *The GDD will create an environment that will enable us to trust others and make true peace in the world community.* It will emphasize unity as our duty in our daily life style. It will help us to see that we and the cultures that have emerged over the eons are not perfect, and that we must think critically and work hard to bring harmony to the globe.

Nothing is permanent. Each person's time on earth is limited. Most of us enjoy our lives for an average of only sixty to one hundred years. Whatever we accomplish or earn during our lifetime of hard work, we will leave behind for someone else. We actually do not own anything here. The Creator of this universe owns everything. We are born with nothing; similarly we die without taking anything from earth with us.

So what are we fighting for? And what do we really need?

What do we need?

Each of us needs these basic things:

1. A place to live

2. Food to eat

3. Clothes to wear

4. Transportation to move us about

5. A job to earn money to pay our bills

6. Mother Nature to support our lives

7. Defense to safeguard us.

Numbers one through five are the main issues in our daily lives. To have a better life we work hard for these. Our Creator gives number six to everyone. No one has to work hard for Mother Nature's gifts of air, water, sunlight, trees, and more.

For number seven, people hire bodyguards, companies hire security guards, cities have police departments, and countries have armies, navies, and air forces to protect their regions.

The first five needs are changing constantly. One hundred years ago, humans lived in totally different types of homes than those we are enjoying now. One hundred and fifty years ago, people ate different types of food and wore different styles of clothes. Two hundred years ago, they used other types of transportation than those we are using today. Two hundred and twenty-five years ago, people were employed in different kinds of jobs to earn food or money. Today's homes, food, clothes, cars, and jobs are much better then what we had in the past. And it will be better in the future—if we choose to adapt to the changes that have come upon us.

Mother Nature herself is changing for all kinds of reasons. One big controversy centers on global warming and whether pollution brings changes in the weather. We don't have control over Mother Nature, but we can take control over the safety of our world. The primary model of the above number seven—having a defense to safeguard us—has not changed that much. Each country still uses its own army, navy, and air force to protect its area. Yes, it is true that today we have better weapons and technology, but the main theory of guarding a nation has not changed at all. *In order for all civilizations on earth to have a better, more peaceful life, we must change the basic concepts involved in how we accomplish number seven.*

20

The Oil-Rich Middle East

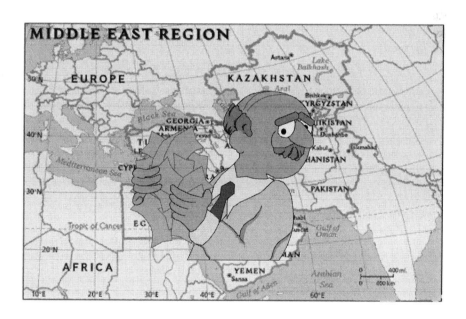

WHY DO MOST TERRORISTS COME FROM the oil-rich countries of the Middle East? The answer is easy. Most of the world's *oil* comes from Middle East. Another name for oil is *black gold*. Western countries need a lot of this black gold to support their highly developed, growing economies. In order to get oil from the Middle East, Western countries have played war games with them to increase their influence, their oil related investments, and their political power.

In the past, England, France, Germany, and the Soviet Union all sent their uniformed troops and weapons into the Middle East. Now, along with the British and French and a host of smaller nations, America is sending advanced weapons and uniformed troops to the Middle East to destroy terrorists. So, we can see that Western countries send their troops and advanced weapons to the Middle East for different reasons.

There are groups of citizens in the Middle East who do not welcome foreign uniformed troops, advanced weapons, and Western countries' political influence and culture into their own land. These groups become one with those terrorists whose aim it is to destroy Western nations. The majority of the people in the Middle East are Muslim; because of that, most of the terrorists are Muslim. By far the greater number of Islamic people do not support terrorism, and the religion itself does not support it. Islam establishes peace, not destruction. Terrorism is actually the reflection of the wars and foreign influence of the last eighty-five years in those countries.

But terrorism is spreading to normal, healthy people like a virus spreads. I believe that together we can stop this virus affecting healthy life in our societies via the GDD.

And this is very important: we should not point fingers at an entire society or religion and identify it as terrorist. Name-calling between whole societies must end—that is, it must if we really want to establish an environment that encourages unity. Calling a nation, a society, or a religion *terrorist* will only fuel ignorance, anger, and stubbornness.

And we must be careful of the way we phrase our aims. When we speak of *war* against terrorism, we are using fighting language and by it actually creating more terrorists who are very willing to fight back. Also embedded in these words is the message that we cannot stop terrorism without more war and violence. This is simply not so! *War and terrorism create a deadly, unending circle, and destroy both humans and nations.*

The superpower countries are spending billions of dollars in war, hoping to win the hearts and minds of Muslims abroad. *But at gunpoint, no one can win any human being's heart or mind. To win the hearts and minds of all humanity, we must change our methods. The concept of the GDD can take us far in that direction.*

"Who are the most dangerous terrorists?"

To find the answer, please read this entire proposal …

21

Why Do Persons Become Terrorists?

PEOPLE COMMIT TERRORIST ACTS WHEN they feel anger, extreme dislike, jealousy, desperation, helplessness, loneliness, and when they lose their families, businesses, real estate, or jobs. Others may become terrorists because they have been the subjects of racial hatred, religious hatred, or they may do it to obtain their own political demands. We see these types of behaviors in people after war, sudden terrorists attacks or political changes. Some join terrorist groups when they do not have the basic needs of life—home, food, clothes, and job.

A person does not have to be a member of a terrorist group or a certain age in order to commit terrorist acts. The truth is that anybody can become a terrorist in his or her own mind, and then when he does, he takes action. But we may say this: *the most dangerous terrorist groups are those who are angry because of another country's power, or its religious and political influence in their country and in their lives.* If they are frustrated in their efforts to find the solution to their problem by peaceful means, they try to destroy the power that is oppressing them. If a stalked animal is cornered, it turns and tries to destroy its pursuer. Even so with humans—in such cases, terrorism seems to them to be the only way.

Terrorism is a global issue, and there are terrorists from every race, religion, and nation. When one strikes out against another who is seen to be an enemy of his people, his people think of him as a hero protecting his country, race, or religion against an oppressor. It is his *enemy* who thinks of him as a terrorist. So who is a terrorist and who is not depends on one's point of view.

What I am saying is that weapon power and technology is not the only solution to terrorism. *Terrorists are humans with a grievance, not enemies that we need more advanced weapons to defeat.* Terrorism is a crisis of the human spirit, and needs a spiritual solution. It is my belief that the GDD can find solutions more spiritual and more friendly to the human spirit.

"How can we avoid war and violence between nations in the twenty-first century?"

To find the answer, please read the entire proposal …

22

Terrorist Attacks

IT WAS IN RESPONSE TO THE TERRORISTS' destruction of the World Trade Center that superpower nations attacked in Afghanistan and Iraq. Because of that terrorist act and the wars that have followed, lots of innocent people have lost their lives. Now people are continuing to lose families, homes, businesses, and jobs. Only a very small percentage of these victims belong to any terrorist group.

Here in the USA, a lot of people have also lost families, jobs, and businesses. Those who have lost loved ones will never fully recover, but as a nation, in other ways, America is recovering very well. Though our lives in the USA are not the same any longer, we still are watching TV, and as we watch, we are hearing more terrorist threats. As a result of this, after 9/11, the way American citizens understand other world societies has changed.

And surely we must see by now that attacking other countries has not and will not likely ever end the violence. Do we not see that in reality, war creates even greater numbers of terrorists, not only in the affected countries, but also in the entire world community? The primary reason for our going to war may not at all have been to stop global terrorism. When it is believed by those in the Middle East that the war had other, secret, motivations, terrorist activity naturally rises. It may be that the terrorists took action against London in the year 2005 because they believed the motivation of the Western countries was other than what we claimed it was.

I love being an American, and I am sickened and horror-struck by those who perpetrated 9/11 in New York and struck on July 7, 2005, in London. So as you can see, I desperately want this vicious cycle to stop!

"How Can We Win the Terrorist Heart and Mind Without Violence?"

To find the answer, please read the entire proposal ...

23

Future Terrorist Attacks

PRESENTLY, NO ONE CAN PREDICT WHEN, where, and how terrorists will attack next. When terrorists blew up two great buildings in New York City using a commercial airliner, few had guessed that such a thing could happen. *Not only did it kill thousands and damage real estate and businesses in the United States, it also affected the entire world economy.*

Preventing terrorism is similar to protecting our cities and towns from natural disasters like Hurricane Katrina in New Orleans or from the earth's movement under the sea that created a tsunami and destroyed a part of Indonesia. In order to find out when, where, and how a natural disaster may strike requires a global monitoring system that is in place everywhere. Many such highly sophisticated sensors exist in the oceans of the world. In the same way, the GDD will keep an eye all over our world on the beginnings of war and terrorism.

While the United States of America and some United Nations countries are carrying on the fight against global terrorism and billions of dollars are been spent to create advanced weapons and new technologies to locate terrorists and bring them to justice, we are left to ask if it could happen again. Are we safe? No one knows for sure. To become more secure, we need anti-terrorism protection such as the GDD that I am proposing can provide.

Terrorist violence looms large on our horizon. Let us spend some time now to study what the last two centuries' wars have brought us and how we can meet the challenge in a better way. It is my belief that the GDD will establish peace between all nations on earth and prevent further loss of lives at home and abroad.

Even though we carried the fight against terrorism into Afghanistan and Iraq, there are threats coming from Iran and Korea. Who knows what country will challenge us next? For worldwide peace, building these wars must stop.

Together we can prevent further violence through the GDD.

"How Can We Stop Creating Terrorists?"

To find the answer, please read the entire proposal …

24

Who is Accountable for Global Terrorism?

PERHAPS WE FIND THE ANSWER to this question is a story from BBC News World Editions—published 2005/07/20 11:12:08 GMT

Mayor blames Middle East policy

"Decades of British and American intervention in the oil-rich Middle East motivated the London bombers, Ken Livingstone has suggested."

The London mayor told BBC News he had no sympathy with the bombers and he opposed all violence. But he argued that the attacks would not have happened had Western powers left Arab nations free to decide their own affairs after World War I. Instead, they had often supported unsavory governments in the region.

"A lot of young people see the double standards," said Ken Livingstone, London Mayor.

Mr. Livingstone was asked on BBC Radio 4's Today program what he thought had motivated the bombers. He replied: "I think you've just had 80 years of western intervention into predominantly Arab lands because of the western need for oil…. We have propped up unsavory governments; we have overthrown ones we did not consider sympathetic And I think the particular problem we have at the moment is that in the 1980s … the Americans recruited and trained Osama Bin Laden, taught him how to kill, to make bombs, and set him off to kill the Russians and drive them out of Afghanistan. They didn't give any thought to the fact that once he'd done that he might turn on his creators."

No justice?

Mr. Livingstone said Western governments had been so terrified of losing their fuel supplies that they had kept intervening in the Middle East. He argued: "If at the end of the First World War we had done what we promised the Arabs, which was to let them be free and have their own governments, and kept out of Arab affairs, and just bought their oil, rather than feeling we had to control the flow of oil, I suspect this wouldn't have arisen."

"British voters don't vote in elections on foreign policy, and suicide bombers won't change this," Andrew, Cirencester, UK

He attacked double standards by Western nations, such as the initial welcome given when Saddam Hussein came to power in Iraq. There was also the "running sore" of the Palestinian/Israeli conflict. "A lot of young people see the double standards, they see what happens in Guantanamo Bay, and they just think that there isn't a just foreign policy," said Mr. Livingstone.

Suicide bombers

Mr. Livingstone said he did not just denounce suicide bombers.

He also denounced "those governments which use indiscriminate slaughter to advance their foreign policy, as we have occasionally seen with the Israeli government bombing areas from which a terrorist groups will have come, irrespective of the casualties it inflicts, women, children and men."

He continued: "Under foreign occupation and denied the right to vote, denied the right to run your own affairs, often denied the right to work for three generations, I suspect that if it had happened here in England, we would have produced a lot of suicide bombers ourselves."

Mr. Livingstone also criticized parts of the media for giving too much publicity to certain figures who were "totally unrepresentative" of British Muslims.

NewsVOA.com
Voice of America
22 July 2005

The rash of suicide bombings in Iraq and the suicide attacks in London earlier this month have focused attention on the motivation for such attacks and how to prevent them. A new study examines hundreds of suicide attacks and why individuals kill themselves to murder others.

University of Chicago Professor Robert Pape has collected evidence and developed a database on more than 300 suicide attacks that have occurred around the world since 1980.

Mr. Pape is the director of the Chicago Project on Suicide Terrorism. During a recent appearance on the VOA public affairs program, Press Conference USA, Mr. Pape says his research indicates that every major suicide campaign has what he calls a secular and political goal, to compel democracies to withdraw military forces from areas the bombers view as their territory.

"Iraq is a prime example of the strategic logic of suicide terrorism. Before the American invasion in March 2003, Iraq never experienced a suicide terrorist attack in its history. Since the invasion of 2003, suicide terrorism has been growing rapidly. Suicide terrorism has doubled in Iraq every year that 140,000 American combat forces have been stationed in the country, and we are on pace now to set a new record for the year."

Mr. Pape says suicide terrorism is not primarily a product of Islamic fundamentalism, although he says religion is used as a recruiting and fundraising tool. He says the world's leading suicide terrorist group is the Tamil Tigers, a secular Hindu group in Sri Lanka. Mr. Pape says the Tamil Tigers have committed more suicide attacks than the Palestinian militant groups Hamas and Islamic Jihad. He says the objective of compelling countries to withdraw military forces from territory the terrorists perceive as occupied has been the central goal of suicide campaigns in Lebanon, Israel, Sri Lanka and among separatists in the Russian republic of Chechnya and the disputed region of Kashmir, which is divided between India and Pakistan.

"Suicide terrorism is mainly a response to the presence of foreign military troops; it is mainly a response to the threat of foreign occupation, not Islamic fundamentalism," he said. "This is a terribly important finding, because it means that the use of heavy military force to transform Muslim societies is only likely to increase suicide terrorists coming at us."

Mr. Pape says his study of hundreds of suicide bombers who actually killed themselves to kill others indicates that most are educated and do not fit the common profile of a person who engages in self-destructive behavior. "What you see is that very few fit the standard stereotype of a depressed, lonely individual on the margins of society seeking to escape some wretched existence. That is, very few are suicidal in the ordinary sense of that term. Instead, most are socially integrated, productive members of their community," he said.

Mr. Pape says that to defeat suicide terrorism, the United States should return to what he calls offshore balancing in the Persian Gulf area. He says that during the 1970's and 1980's, the United States successfully managed its interests in the region by not permanently stationing troops in Muslim countries, but maintaining the ability to rapidly deploy military forces to hot spots when necessary.

Mr. Pape says the United States should develop the same strategy to defeat suicide terrorism in Iraq. "Over the next year, we should transfer responsibility for Iraq's army to the Iraqi government, and then we should begin a systematic withdrawal of ground forces, not in a hasty way, but, so (that), over the next two or three years, we transition to a situation, where the Iraqi government is in charge of its army, and the United States has excellent relations with that new government," he said.

Mr. Pape has presented his findings to members of the U.S. Congress, and hopes his research will help policymakers as they continue efforts to boost the nation's defenses against suicide terrorism. There has been no immediate response from Congressional leaders to Mr. Pape's findings.

Author's Note

My motivation …

YOU MAY WONDER WHY I have written this book and what my motivation is for wanting to establish the GDD.

My motivation is very strong. In the past, I have known war. In the present, I have been angry and saddened by the conflict in the world and the toll it is taking on lives and human happiness. It is out of love for humanity and a wish to help others escape this terrible dilemma that I want to establish in our environment the WWP and GDD. With these, I believe we can avoid war, stop global terrorism, and much of the rampant destruction of Mother Nature on our earth can be brought to an end.

We humans want to follow where duty and responsibilities lead us. When we go to work for a company, we like to see that a scope of work exists for each employee. Every successful company on earth has some kind of highly developed system that all employees follow. *Now if we can initiate the GDD scheme for all humans on earth, entire future generations will be born and grow up in that system and in a peaceful world.*

We should come to understand that none of the Middle East governments are terrorist governments, but terrorism has become a human crisis in our society and in other societies worldwide.

It is clear that terrorists cannot defeat the advanced weapons and technology of the twenty-first century. But we should find it equally clear that advanced weapons cannot wipe out global terrorists. So what can we do? You now know my answer.

Epilogue

The GDD at UN   **Our World Leaders**

I HAVE A SPECIAL REQUEST to make of all superpower leaders, of the United Nations officers, and of all terrorists: SUPPORT THE GDD PROJECT SO THAT EVERY CITIZEN MAY HAVE A PEACEFUL LIFE ON OUR EARTH. I believe that the only way we can better ourselves as a world community is to work together through the GDD for the defense of all our countries.

Together, let us work toward this goal of promoting the Global Defense Department for the purpose of securing unity in our global society.

In the twenty-first century, people, ways of life, business models, and weapons meant to defend nations are changing. Using traditional ways, we cannot protect our nation any more.

The GDD will create an atmosphere in which we may work as TEAM, not only in the United States of America but also with all countries.

Working as partners in defense is the best way to protect every nation in today's global society. The GDD will elevate the relationships between all countries. It will become the one-stop center for global defense.

We need also to remind ourselves, young as well as old that the solution to our war and terrorism problems and concerns lie in following and sticking to the noble disciplines that will be outlined by the Global Defense Department.

The divisions between us are the biggest problem we have worldwide. No case on earth can justify the killing of innocent civilians, no matter how much injustice and oppression one has been subjected to. The GDD initiative at the United Nations is not intended for the benefit of one country and culture alone, but for the benefit of the entire world. It is an organization that will make us stronger, not weaker. And it will keep us safe!

Not only will it keep us safe, it will also protect global economy and trade as it emerges in the twenty-first century.

Author

This book will present you with the key concept of establishing in the United Nations a Global Department of Defense—The GDD—and it will set forth our need for a global security force. Once WE initiate GDD with your assistance, we will create an Internet web site with everything detailed. You will discover how your money is working for your peace and your comfort on earth.

I propose to the international community that we work towards the establishment of the Global Defense Department (GDD) at the United Nations for the preservation of peace settlements in all the world's areas of conflict. I pray to God almighty to bless all the people of the world with his peace and mercy.

Here is a question for all people who talk about peace: what are you doing to stop all terrorist activities and the killing of more innocent people and the increase in terror? Please read this GDD proposal for the answers that you have been looking for: how and why people are becoming terrorists and what we can do to stop war, violence, and terrorists attacks.

Each human being, culture, and nation is unique on our earth, therefore, it is important to respect one another and learn from each other to avoid these conflicts. Conflict between nations is the initiator of war and fuels terrorist anger.

All the countries of the world should pool their defense budgets and have a world army or global security force to deal with all world conflicts.

What You Will Discover from this Worldwide Peace Proposal …

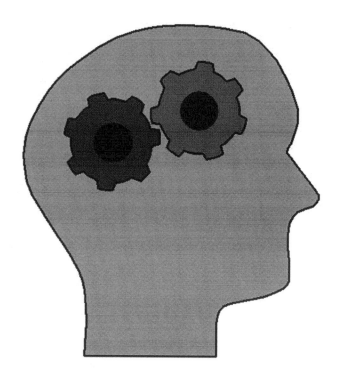

- How to initiate global peace through the United Nations

- Why we need to unite as a team in a UN Global Defense Department

- How to safeguard each nation in the twenty-first century

- How to establish peace between nations

- How to work with superpower leaders at the United Nations

- Why Western countries are interested in the Middle East crisis

- Why terrorists come from the Middle East

- Why most known terrorists are Muslim

- Why terrorists attack superpower countries

- How to win terrorists' minds and hearts

- Who is accountable for global terrorism

- How to stop creating further terrorists around the world

- Which nations spend one third of their national budgets to create weapons of mass destruction

- Why advanced weapons cannot stop global terrorism

- What the relationship between war and terrorism is

In God we trust. God Bless the United States of America and our World!

978-0-595-42262-3
0-595-42262-4

10985157R00057

Made in the USA
Lexington, KY
03 October 2018